# Poetical Contemplation

**AGNES RAMYA SRILATHA PALAPARTHI**

# Dedication

To me ,
From my
Imagination of deep
thoughts .

# Contents

93. AN OVER WHELMING

94. I STAND TOWERING

95. CUMULUS CLOUDS

.96. YOUR'RE THE

97. AS I WOKE UP

98. RUNNING OUT

99. ME ON THE OTHER WORLD 100. IM STUCK

101. I LOOK UP TO YOU

102. CURRENTLY

103. STUCK

104. BARE FEET

105. DESTINY & FATE

106. OUT OF LOVE

107. IN A BOX

108. TOO MANY THINGS

109. AN IMMOVABLE STATUE

110. AS I RETURN

111. SHABBY ROADS

.112. WE HOLD

113. A WILD FLOWER

114. A COMPANION TO TREAT .

115. TWLIGHT LIGHT

116. THERE ARE TWO MANY

# And Perhaps !

And perhaps what made her
"*beautiful*"
was not her
"*appearance* "
or what she is ,
but
in her
*love,*
in her
*courage*
in her Audacity to
*believe* .

No matter the
darkness around her ,
light ran within her .
And that was the way she came
"*alive*".
&
it showed up everything!

# I Used to Find Myself !

I used to find

myself

*in the reflection*

*of water,*

cleansing myself from,

the TROUBLED thoughts .

Waves of HAPPINESS

Waves of JOY

Waves of BEING LONELY

Waves of EXCITEMENT

Waves of NUMBNESS

that all comes in

*"waves".*

# As I make a Twirl !

As i make a twirl,
*the bliss of*
*shining sky ,*
*makes a sprinkle*
of whisper with the words .
I dreamt
& believed to be impossible ,
which turns out be a masterpiece .

With the gleaming gold of
precious threshing  sun ,
You
*Carved me into a*
*perfect*
*imperial character,*
spinning to the infinity & beyond .

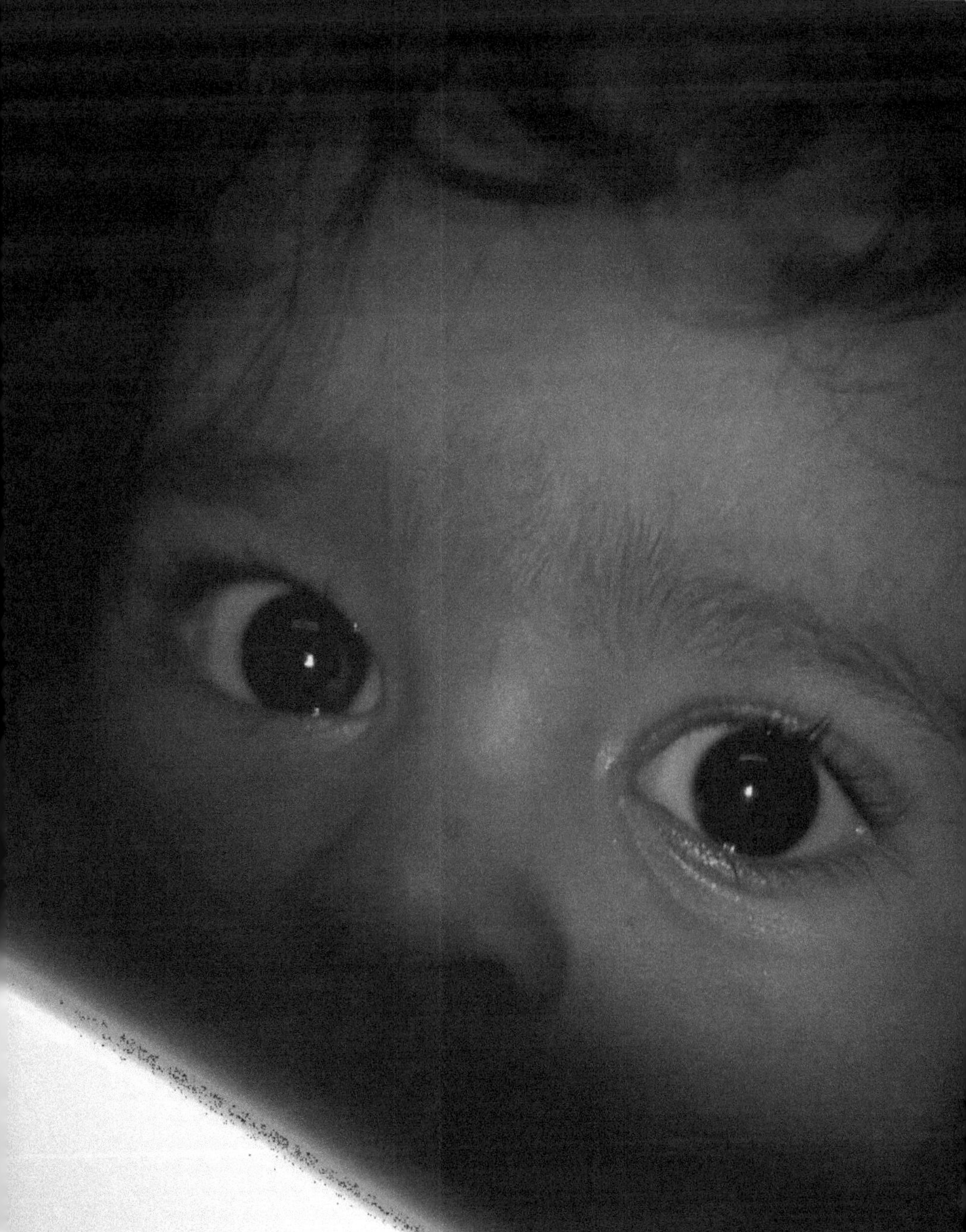

# Staring Into Your're eyes !

Staring into you're eyes ,
*Enlightens my soul ,*
Forgetting the world aside .

The pupil of you're eye ,
Shines like a sparkling moon,
*Brightening
my tiny heart ,*
With the enrapturing relish .

You're pretty almond eyes ,
Whispers the untold amour ,
Of the covalent bond between
*YOU & ME .*

# Renewed By !

Renewed by birth ,
turning into a beauty that
"PRESIDES".


The Transformation that
reforms ,
Gives a hope  for
"NEW LIFE ".


The undefined colours of
your wings,
emblem the meaning of
"HEAVEN".


The impulsive bravery you show,
gives the energy to express
one's
"EMPOWERMENT".

# Alluring flowers !

Alluring flowers which makes me,

Tend to fall to greet,

as ,

I cannot rhyme a song

On her beauty just to
Enchant.

The things that bounce which ,

are not sufficient to profound,

as the beauty that is reflected

deep within me,

is picked by the way she is !

# Everything

Everything has a limit
To the love you
show,
To the care you
bow .
Nothing changes
if we stopped
our souls for a while,
but the  feeling of lost
hits hard for a while .


Question the clock whats
the crime,
An unknown silence folded
the sublime .

Every

*hour*

Every

*second,*

Every

*minute,*

reminds the

tricking time we spend .

Accepting the

*frill,*

emphasising the

*still.*

limiting the heart to

*kill,*

burying the

will of everything .

# A Pleasant Evening!

It's a pleasant evening ,
*the bliss of*
*peacefulness*
evaded her.
The birds going to
their nests ,
welkin turning to
tiny droplets.
A warm cup of
Americano in hands,
The prose on the lap
*tranquil her.*
It looked up like
the perfect instant moment ,
for her mentality.

# I See You

I See You
*not like the world see you*
I look up with a tender heart ,
Seeking the gentle warmth you might grant.

I See You
*through my admiring eyes*
Glancing the memories we made .
I gaze at You're soul that relinquishes, My
incarnation.

I See You
*beyond the tint of green,*
that adds beauty to the sky.

I See You
*through You're Wholesome,*
that makes my life full sum.

# Poetry is !

Poetry is
"FOCUSING"
on , a scene or an event .
"CAPTURING"
it with your "EYES"
"PROCESSING"
it in your "MIND"
"FEELING "
it in your "HEART"
&
"EXPRESSING"
it with your "WORDS".

# My Moon !

Oh My Denoting love,
You're the light to my wildest
*darkness,*
Pearly silver lining to my
*loneliness.*
Solitary among those
*stars,*
Shining deeper to see the
*jars.*

The brightening of those
little charms
Make me wander in
your blaze ,
Your gleeful shape of crescent ,
Adds beauty to the welkin.

Enchanting the gaiety of you
fullness
is admired on the
liveness .
*You're called as Chandini,*
which brings elegance to the galaxy.

You're my companion for the
*dimnes*
showing dimensions to my
*gloominess* .
Giving a rhythm to my melody ,
Tuning it into
*chandamama* .


Shrugging out of the clouds ,
illustrates a bond between us .
Warming my
heart through your
*light,*
surrounded by your tight .


Peeping throughout my life,
*moon you have been my boon for
this life .*

# Heart Full of

Heart full of unwinding
*melody*,
Rhyming the unknown
*remedy*.
Blushing Through
the little moments
with the twinkling
*eyes*,
An chords tuned the
*arise.*
Mesmerising the memories
that created in the
*cerebrum*,
flourishing the soul in this
contemporary
*bum.*
Heart full of unwinding
*melody*
Rhyming the unknown
*memory..*

# Let Me

Let me be

*you're twinkler*

in

*you're existence,*

like the dazzling stars

in the  sky.

# Ohmyyyyyyy!

Oh My Sunset ,
You're aura still lingers .
A Charming Shade
across the SKY ,
A Perfect way of
Getting back to FLY  .
The First sign of day
waving good bye ,
Beautifying
you're colours that paint
the sky .
Flashing of the
brightening HUES,
Leaving the traces on the BLUES .

# She has a  !

She has a Crescent
*Eyes like the moon,*
She talks like the
Sprinkle drops of rain .
She has a Messy Hair ,
Mesmerising in an artful way .

She dressed up in Cherry red
like the Red Champagne ,
Admiring the Ravishing gloom
of her charm ,
Through the never
ending prospective vision .

# Clearing off


Clearing off
the
*Circumstances*
&
Concentrating
on the
exploit ,
Makes You're conscious
*worth while.*

# As I Rise !

As i Rise my wings ,
The sting of penury in my heart ,
Strengthen's my soul .

The flashes of the
Fantasy ,
Reminds of the
deeper gloom of tragedy .

Heedless of the insisted Cells ,
Hushed  the melody to
Bloom in Dwells .

# The Welkin is !

The Welkin is
Flushed with the Dawn
&
*My path lies beautiful*
along with the
Lawn .

# Clouds !

Clouds
I sometimes stare at you .
The Residents of the sky ,
The Rulers of the vast gloom.
Constantly travelling ,
Taking various shapes & sizes ,
Small Patches ,
Big Formation .
Twilighting  the Flamingo ,
with the IRIDESCENT &
PEARLESCENT glittering .

# Strolled Fired up !

Strolled fired up in the
Mid sunny day ,
A ray of Viridescent
of Crust ,
Shielding to the glossy
Golden Treasure
That recline beneath .

The summer
enlightenment placed ,
below the welkin .
All through the sweetness about ,
blasting away the taste bud
is
explosion of being the
" THE KING OF FRUITS ".

THE NEW YOU
Katzen
Graphen
LADIES AND GENTLEMEN

# The Retro

The Retro vintage
*of her,*
stroll around the
corner of evergreen .
flipping through
the endless laughter of
*blush,*
creating the aroma of 90's .
Her enlightened eyes
evoked the memories of
*a Porcelain look .*
The pompadour hairstyle
made her iconically pretty .
The alluring attire of her ,
made her astonished for decades,
*remembering the vintages .*

# EVERYTHING IS !

Everything is frozen up,

The Wind & The Breeze.

The bliss of the shining clouds & stars

*hanged out in Frost.*

The Silent whispers of the moon ,

Tackled with  the Tune .

# Hey There !

Hey there
Ray of sunshine .
Time to wakeup,
come out
& play .
Breaking through
the tiny cracks
of a shattered old window ,
Illuminating
where all
darkness resides .
Brushing away
all the grey
and pain of yesterday ,
Warm rosy cheeks,
&
the cold sleepy  face of  today .

# You Made me

You Made me
*laugh love & live*
which truly cherished my heart
*for this lifetime.*
It made me to reborn
in the fondness of being
original to you .
Yet,
Everything disparated
like the,
soap bubble prick .
Hard to accept
Sad to learn
the unchangeable reality ,
It's the smile
that can switch the soul ,
which holds back
the rallying to get
the covalent bond .

# It Is A
# Windy Day !

It is a windy day !
The girl and her kite
Fought against the wind ,
To fly  high ,
in the Fictional  incarnation .
Same in the Reflection
Of her thoughts ,
She flourished
to enchant her
Aspirations,
with a
Daisy chains of drift,
Like the ,
Rise of phoenix
from the ashes.

# An Enigmatic Smile

An Enigmatic Smile she dressed ,
to enchant mystery .
she's been decked ,
with love & kindness .

The bliss of shine,
in her eyes ,
to apprise the
charm of existence .

The ultimate unfolding story ,
behind the blissful smile ,
is a silver of hope ,
to bloom without clues .

# Hand in Hand

Hand in Hand ,
Shoulder to Shoulder .
An unknown Frequency
Bind together .
Cheering up throughout the
*lifetime,*
Calling them as mine
*all time* .
They are defined as the Meaning of
*"friends like family".*

# Like the Foam

Like the Foam

*that fills the water,*

Sadness covered me .


Finding the love again

*where i lost,*

But a foam of heart break

*remained frost.*

# My Mask Is !

My Mask is pretty yah !
*serenity ,*
*insanity ,*
it got all the best over it .
From Gleaming
*sadness ,*
to covering the blushing
*smiles .*

It buried all the darkness ,
within me .
It not only saved me from
the determinal alignment
but ,
reminds me
to keep myself secured
from the countless tears .

# Draping

Draping beautifully like a doll ,
in her chaos .
She is like a
Trilling snow Flake ,
fallen behind
without any Trail .
She invaded into the crown
Drip  into  conflit ,
Adhering the mysterious gleam
about her.
She trickles a striking spril
like a money plant ,
yearns from
the shattering
pieces of life .

# Lost Into !

Lost into the world
where everything,
seems to be lovely .
The Heart feels
DELIGHT .
The Mind blowing
BRIGHT .
Covered with the sight of
EXICTE.
Enchanted by the
TWILIGHT .

Driven into
PARADISE .
Surrounded by the gentle Air .
Widening the shattered wings ,
To sweep the Untiring
FLIGHT .
Realising it late ,
I have lost into an imaginary
TIGHT .

# I'm Like

I'm Like a solitary bird

in the welkin,

*you're my fluttering*

solitude to my dusk.

# Take Me !

Take me ,
To the place that gives me
"*peace* ".

Take me,
To the world that shows only
"*love*".

Take me ,
To the skies ,
where i rise my wings
&
Sings a soulful song for you .
Take me to the a
galaxies that amazes our
"*magic*".

Take me ,
Beyond the seas ,
that  enchant
the flow of amore within us .

# The Mind

The Mind  full of
*stress,*
thinking about the worldly
*mess.*
tendered as broken
*glass,*
lying with the pieces of
*grass.*


The Huddles & Struggles
of this span ,
Squawking the heart han .
The intellectual wits are
filled by
*selfishness,*
making the pit of others
*owness.*

This is only for you
or
the world is in the way,
flowing through
the flow of life
is harder day by day .
when can i get a peaceful feeling of today .

it's only you
&
you have to be you
to survive in this circle of
you !

# Where Am I ?

Where am i ?
What am i ?
How i'm supposed to be ?
Running our of mind ,
Wondering about the
multiples .
Million of unanswered
questions ,
With shitty reasons
To stable the heart .

Breathing
Reaching
Catching
&
Dreaming
What after all life is !

# A Coral

A Coral Georgette Saree
with the rhyming of a

beautiful neck piece .

Her golden sunshine portrait ,

Gloriously makes her
Alluring.

The Fairy innocence of blush ,

adds sparkle

to the admiring one .

The viridescent of amalgamation

made her glitter ,

in the fragrance of

art of being

pretty visually deep within her .

# Million

Million of

Brightening stars ,

But i admire

for that damn one,
that shines for me.

# Fixing The

Fixing the
*broken soul,*
Dipped in a
*Sorrow full roll.*
Cranky ,
Cringy whole ,
Playing across the Droll.

Fixing the
broken soul ,
Strolling in a mood
of console.
Hit ,
Fit ,
Into transmit ,
Engaging into a  perfect bit .

# Being solace

Being solace to one side,
and stirring it on the other side ,
does it make any sense .
Keeping the emotions with solitary ,
dripping into another side ,
does it make any sense .

Ensuring that people are
"two faced"
like a rattle snake ,
they may be on the same boat
but ,
The deception of the plot counts .

Honeyed words & fishhook barbs,
lies within them .
Disgusied as candy bar ,
crosses behind your back
as masked up propinquity .

# The sun

The sun
*rises tentatively ,*
through the forest heights ,
*behind the spot.*
The sanctuary of wilderness
louden its voice
to the admiring  nature .
The sunshine in the calm rays ,
*dews sparkle*
on tender grasses .
The Rain has washed
the delicate leaves,
where ferns dance ,
through the cool breze,
*that blow through love .*

# Dozing

Dozing all day ,
without doing nothing
is currently
*a new vibe of mine.*
Laying like a
potato couch ,
passing the time
with the glass of wine
*is a new vibe of mine.*
Having No mood for
a single thing
being good for nothing ,
*is a new vibe of mine.*

# Not Everyone

Not everyone has a
*heart like you*
Not everyone has a
*thought like you.*
Not everyone could be

she

as she is a

*bomb shell*

made of

*dynamite.*

She turned to be

invincible by

impending the threads of ,

*blind fold.*

to bring a change  in her ,

she altered into

*Annabelle.*

# She Bloomed

She bloomed
*like a*
*pretty*
*glimmering flowers,*
A beautiful soul
designated for herself .
Sweet as sugar ,
Portraying on the vision .
The authentic ,
ethral will be you,
Holding the tincture ,
of arrogance &
*surrounded*
*with heavenly grace .*

# The Fluffiest

The fluffiest clouds
makes me
spellbound ,
when you're  with me .
The magic that
invaded in me ,
makes me fall for you ,
again & again .
enchanting the eye sight
of yours
gives a reason
to live .

# Walking Through

Walking through the
*greenery path,*
soothing me
the enchanting
feeling of aroma,
which awakens my soul.

The rewinding tincture
gives me the ,
refreshment to
my persistence.
The grassy touch to my
bare feet ,
makes exaltation to my
spirit ,
arising the sense  of
delight.

# Sailing !

Sailing through
up & downs in life
Standing at the
mid point of view ,
Reminding me
what the existence is !

Living life in the
simplest Pleasures
worthing the Leasures .
*Essentilising*
the own mind
*moulding*
the world aside .
Enjyoing the little things ,
Waving the natures wings .

# The Tiny

The Tiny droplets of water

that falls on the

*petals,*

makes them

*reinvigorate.*

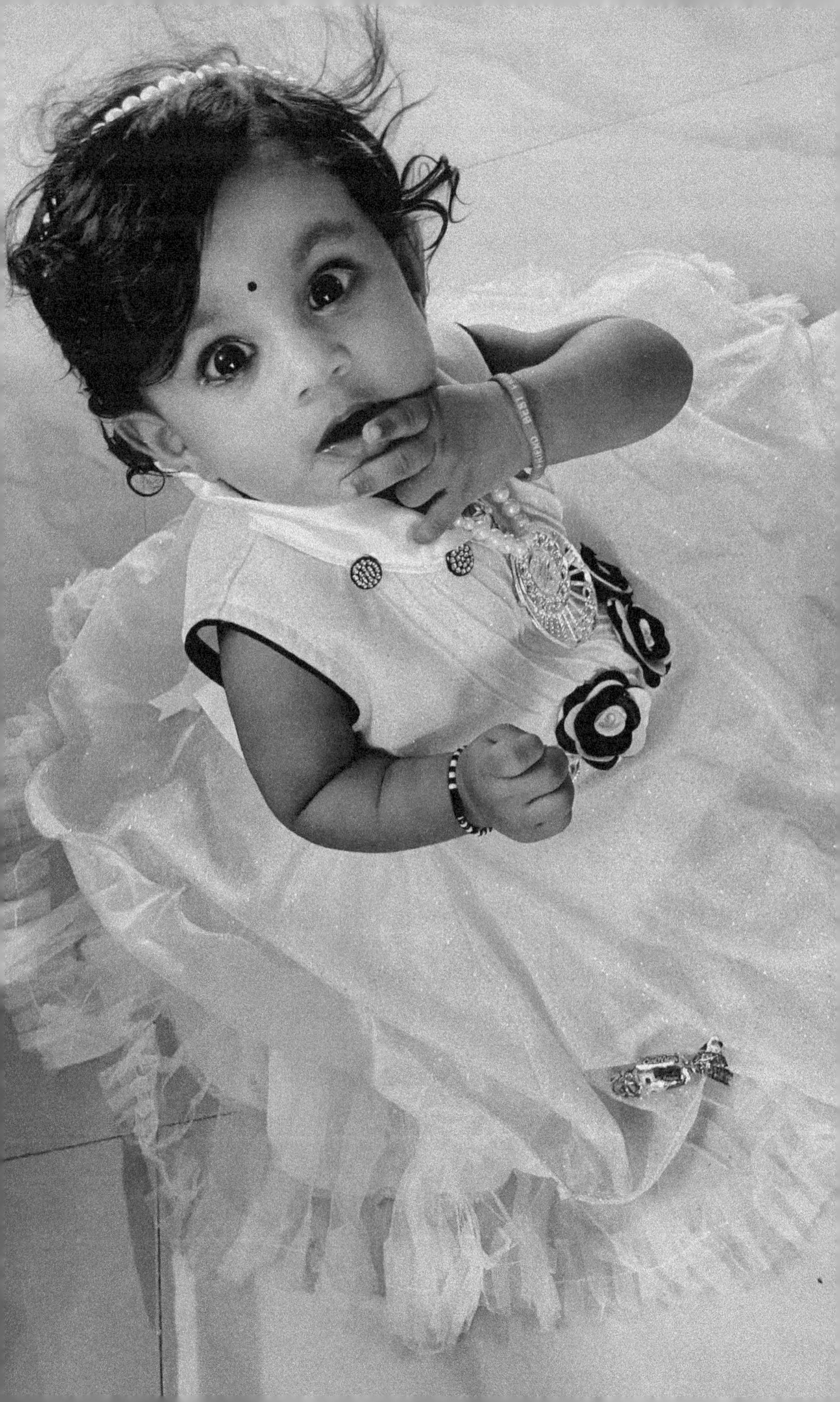

# Eyes !

Eyes !
The  Beguited beauty of  you .
They are like the toasted
" *hazel nut* "
light brown & pretty often .

The luminescent  bindi
on your face ,
brings life .
Quizzed with the words
your eyes speak ,
vocalising the deep within.

Glazing the mushy hair,
leaves us to be ,
" *traped* "

# Desperate

Desperate struggle in my
*heart,*
time plays the
*game,*
luck lashes out the
*fame.*
walking through the
*darkness,*
covering with the
*loneliness,*
life seems to  a chess board .
Stuck between the
*grief*
plot seems to be
*brief,*
the Tale of life looks like a
*sheaf.*

# Oh My Pretty !

Oh My pretty
Dandelion ,
tricking ,
threading
the consistency of life ,
through the fragile & fro .

Flying away you're seed ,
one after one ,
through the
brightening nod ,
with the cherishing heart .

The love you sacrifice ,
is profound immensely .
it reminds
that love
is harder than we think.

# Holding the tips !

Holding the tips,
*of your comfy fingers,*
evidently under
the aroma of the greenery .
The gasps of my heart ,
skipped a beat ,
wheezing the sound of
your heart .

The little tiny countenance
blushed enthusiastically
with ,
the utmost joy which ,
enhanced  my soul
with the gesture ,
*reminiscing it for
"lifetime".*

# Waves !

The Waves
*listen to my*
*Mourning whisper,*
consoling through
the tiny soft sand .
The water
sweeps over my feet ,
surrounded by the
bliss of aurora.
The splashes reminds of
the elapsed reminiscent .
convincing myself
to built up
like a robust castle in the ocean !

# She Dressed Up !

She Dressed up
*in confidence & Belief*.
Steering off
the hardest situations
in life,
She turned out to be
a blissful girl.

The Frimly strong base
&
the trails
*made her a*
*warrior by heart*.
She is like an anchorage
made everyone
like an absolute clown.

# Wheels of life !

Lounging at the top of welkin ,
visioning the
moments of amusement rides ,
rotating the upright life .


Running through the
*wheels of life,*
Chasing through the
*dreams of life,*
Shattering through the
*happiness of life .*


Circling Round & Round ,
Reminding that life is a circle ,
ensuring the bravery we face.

# You & Me

You & Me
are like the Mutabilis
with different shades,
of tincture
belonging to one spectrum.
The hidden beauty of your soul
is shining like a shadow of the tree.
The unwinding story of us
is the HIDE & SEEK game
like Mimosa pudica .

# The Monsoon

The  Monsoon of her wrath ,
manufacturing her to
*cuddle & puddle.*
She is living life to the fullest ,
chilling herself
with the succulent
drops of rain .
The sky bringing the ,
*power & prosperity*
for her life ,
exhilarating in wonder.
The blurred reflection
of the wet floor ,
endures the unlimited spirit.
A fending red umbrella
drives the symphonic chaos !

# It's In Her !

It's in her
monarch hair ,
reflected through the
*"golden ray of light"*.
Fluttering like a butterfly,
with sun kissed ,
silken ivory .
Painted the freckles,
conscientious the soul.
Elegance personified
the dazed face ,
like a bright twinkling of the
*"blamy radiance"*.

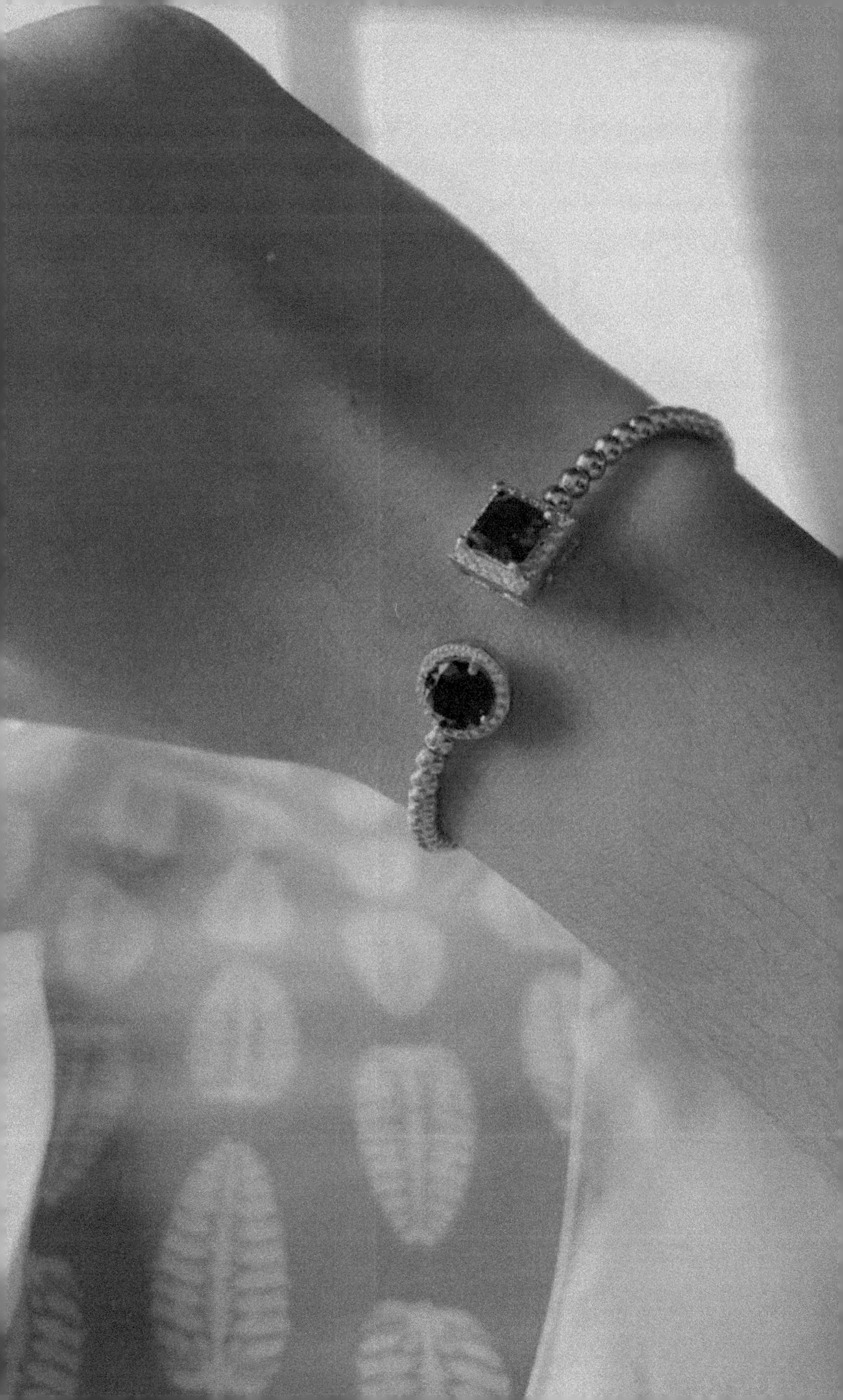

# A Year

A Year<br>
*filled with*<br>
*The unknown feeling in life,*<br>
Where everything changed<br>
into pure magic .<br>
The heart of steel<br>
melted<br>
&<br>
turned out to be beautiful a bud<br>
with tender of intimacy .

The songs of melody<br>
Rhyme the beat of<br>
you're heart,<br>
The lyrics flowed like<br>
the sweetest honey of<br>
you're voice.

# Wah Taj !

The First thing
that hooks the eyes is
*you.*
Your the monument of
*love.*
once in a lifetime
everyone gasps your
*beauty* .
You gave the life's biggest
*happiness,*
that will definitely excels me
throughout my senescence .
It makes me twiril ,
to canvas my heart ,
with the marble touchwood
of tipsy feeling of
*"wah taj".*

# Lay Me !

Lay me hold on to the

*Candyfloss,*

reflecting through the crystal of

*Love.*

# A piece of

A piece of
*unsatisfied melancholy,*
whispering through
the sky .
The impending waves
made an approach ,
to the grounded soul .
The neutralising thoughts
running in  her mind
are like
*tiny pebbles,*
Filling the pot
*To be a better person .*

# You're My

You're my welkin
to my full moon ,
*complete & perfect*
to my lifespan.
Standing in the fondness ,
wrenching to mend
in this cruel world .
Facing all the ups & downs
to withstand
Hoping that,
you could be mine
*forever* .

# Mind

Surly state of
*mind,*
caged with a
billion thoughts of
*bind.*
Unaware of the
tears falling
*behind,*
Encouraging myself to be
*kind.*

Life filled
with misery a
*side,*
Racing with the hope of
*ride.*
Hiding in the dram of
*life,*
Waiting for the turn of
*Drive.*

Dreams blocked at the
*shore,*
Moving around the
*souls,*
Drenching the
*Heart,*
Breathing the
*Reality,*
with a  confused plot .


Playing like

the puppets

&

toys in the stage of life ,
*My Mind*
*is an unstoppable player*
in it .

# You Taught

You Taught

*me the definition of love*

she said ,

You Making me live

to archive what it is

he said .

# Dancing

*Dancing*
through the chaos
of deepest paths ,
winding the universal
illumination aside .
*Singing*
the best through
melancholy divine ,
crossing the edge with the align.

# Lost

Lost on the track of
*life,*
finding them in between to
*strive.*
Building the bricks of
*paradise,*
aligning within the bites of
*wise.*

Facing the
*Criticise,*
Bearing with
*compromise.*
To be a perfect
*poeticise,*
i been devise from the
*arise.*

# The Bliss

The Bliss of the
Glossy Tresses ,
that falls on your brow .
Finger waving
those tresses,
make me tingle ,
the butterflies in my
*tiny little heart.*

The amazement in
your round eyes ,
take this Annabelle
to the other world of existence .
the wings of fondness
gracefully transform into  a
*new life.*

# She's Been

She's been on
*cloud nine,*
so as the
*lightening shine.*
The dream of
*fondness,*
wrenched her to
*bitterness.*
The softness of her
*incarnation,*
turned to be the
*distraction.*
Perhaps the solitary pick
made her to scar
the mark of mini heart break.

# Tearing up

Tearing up every night,
fearing down the lane ,
with a Melancholy mood.

Figuring out on the things
that are
*demolished,*
surviving to
*Accomplish.*
Through many toils & snares
The shattered pieces of Dreams ,
are clinched .

Life became a nightmare
thinking to chase ,
By the trembling thoughts
that run through my head.

# Dazzling

Oh my little tiny
*droplets dazzling*
in the behold ,
quite immense pleasant as
*the motif* .

# A Strength
# you needed to !

A Strength you needed to
To Manage that you're okay,
with a cherishing smile.

A Strength you needed to
To Balance the mood swings ,
where no body can understand .

A Strength you needed to
To pretend in this world,
Where people
are concerned about their own self .

A Strength you needed to
To survive in this worldly world.

Above all,
all you need is a strength
to your mind
to live long !

# You Make

You make
*my heart smile
for the too & fro,*
in the clinging cozy day .
Blushing through the
conversation of love ,
seen in the pearly eyes.

Cheesing to the
comfortable zone
twinkling the
magical vibe ,
with the tincture of
fondness we share.

Admiring the soul full feel ,
Amusing the elegance
you make my heart smile
for the too & fro.

# The Sunny Rays

The Sunny rays of
*clime on hair,*
mesmerising Artfully ,
with pearly Round eyes.
The Tresses are like her attitude ,
*tangled with tender,*
which brings elegance to the castle.
The Untied Hair
Soothens It's follicle by
the blowing wind.
The dimensions of
the incredible shine
*amplified her.*

# There are

There are nights
Where i
*cry alone,*
There are nights ,
Where i
*drown in pain .*

There are nights
Where i
*feel lost,*
There are nights
Where i
*search for sleep .*

There are nights
where i
*suffer in grief*
There are nights
Where i
*deal with sadness*

There are nights
where i
*face the
darkest moments.*
There are nights
Where i'm
*out of words.*

There are nights
where i'm
*speechless*
to express about what
*i been going through.*

157

# Masquerade cruise

Pretending Behind
the wind ,
Hiding a confined fine.
Abiding to remind,
cloaking the carnival night.
Scandalous combined ,
Elegance defined.
Designed in Fantasy ,
Declining the  Identity.
Making history divine ,
Dancing the misery aside .
Breaking the norms & rules,
Gathering to perform the
masquerade cruise .

# Watching

Holding the hands,
Feeling secured among the
stars .
*Watching into you're eyes,*
Making my life
brighter to highs .
Awaiting the hearts to meet ,
Giving the utmost happiness
to the
contemporary .
Blushing under
the luminescence ,
Delighting the existence with
*love.*

# Silent whispers

The silent whispers
*of the wind,*
Reminds me of
You're  thoughts .

The fluffy clouds
*surrounds me,*
with you're knots.

Chasing through
thick's & thins ,
life with you will be the
light of wins.

# Eyes !

Eyes !
The looks that
hooks the heart .
The beauty that
*grabs the attention* .
The reason to skip
a heart beat .
The million of untold folds,
where words fail to express .

Eyes !
*An emotion*
That convey within .
*An enigmatic*
Riddle to figure out .
*An arrow*
That triggers ,
*A Star*
to gaze at
&
*A beauty*
that exist .

AUTO
FILL IN
INTRO
MAIN/VARIATION
STYLE CONTROL
A B C D E

# Immersed

Immersed
*in the art of music,*
My soul
*felt like heaven .*
Playing
a rhythm of song ,
That up
lifts my soul .
The keys
are dipped in honey ,
Sweet & Soothing
To my ears .
The magical sound
makes me free ,
*from all the pain .*

# Looking

Looking out into the millions ,
*I find you.*
Staring into the Dreamscape ,
*I got you.*

ON

# Clinching

Clinching
Between
*the time & consistency,*
Swapping the soul
into a horror lost form .
It's not just a switch ,
to turn on & off
the feeling
& emotions ,
that roll up my life .
But an eternity to rise,
The everlasting love lies
*deep inside my heart.*

# A State Of mind

A State of Mind
*where everything seems*
*to be falling apart.*
Confusion

Insane

In pain

The Cuts

The Scars

Driving me to depart .


An illustration

to death ,

*Breathing*

with suffocation .

*Surviving*

in the stilled water ,

with the stead fast hope.

Unable to change
the things ,
Building
my heart to cage ,
in an ice cold pack.
Cry
Dry
Yet still alive as usual ,
to archive
something in life.

# She Bloomed

She Bloomed
*In the*
*pieces of flaws,*
Adding the fantasy across .
An old soul ,
With the young eyes,
&
A vintage heart.

She is delicate
*so as*
*the pretty petals*
deliberately
trying to be brazen ,
like the
*corals in the sea.*

# Love !

Love !
The 4 word which is
*magical,*
*hard &*
*difficult to find.*
The 4 word that encodes the
*heart, mind & soul.*
The 4 word which is not just a feeling ,
but
*an emotion to live within.*


Love !
The 4 word that twinkles the eyes ,
*like stars.*
The 4 words that make you tickling
*of butterflies,*
The 4 word which is
*valuable,*
yet it is liable to understand .

# A Soul in

A Soul in
*search,*
lost its
*peace,*
Wandering around the
*beach.*
The Sand touching
*my feet,*
Soothing my veins with
*Ticklings.*

Walking,
Washing ,
The heavy heart with the
*tides.*
merged between the
*blues.*

# Lamp light

In the ring of lamplight
His eyes looked bright.
Peering into the darkness ,
summoned with imagination.

Enlightened the flame ,
Burning the lame .
The fog covered him ,
with my love
persisting the pain .

Like the sights & sounds
of a far distant past,
Crossing the portals
of a Million
lost.
Seeing the image of  my human ,
Blown away with the word of
yearning
frost.

The fluency in

*silence,*

covered my soul ,

with calmness .

The crystals of

*white,*

*Serendipitous to my mind.*

The wind melts my

*strife,*

*empowering my body with my*

*soul .*

# You're my

You're my

*perfect tincture,*

to my pretty twilight .

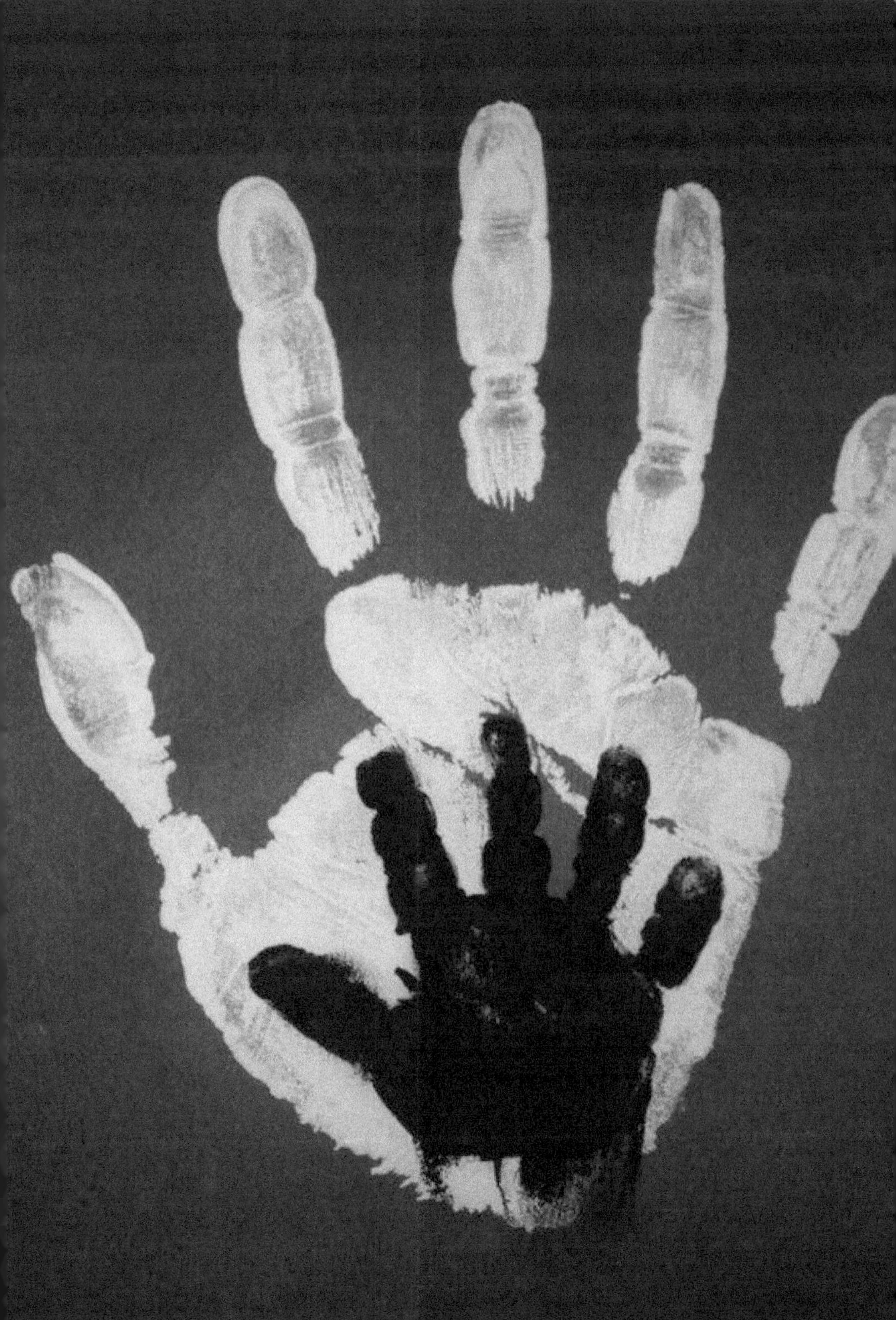

# A Hand

A Hand you  Always need
*To Guide you*
through You're life.
*To Pick you*
in all aspects of You're life .
*To Make you*
a perfect individual ,
&
*To Mould you*
into a good path .

A Hand you Always need
In terms of
*happiness,*
in terms of
*sorrow ,*
in terms of
*broken pieces*
& in terms of
*immensely lost.*

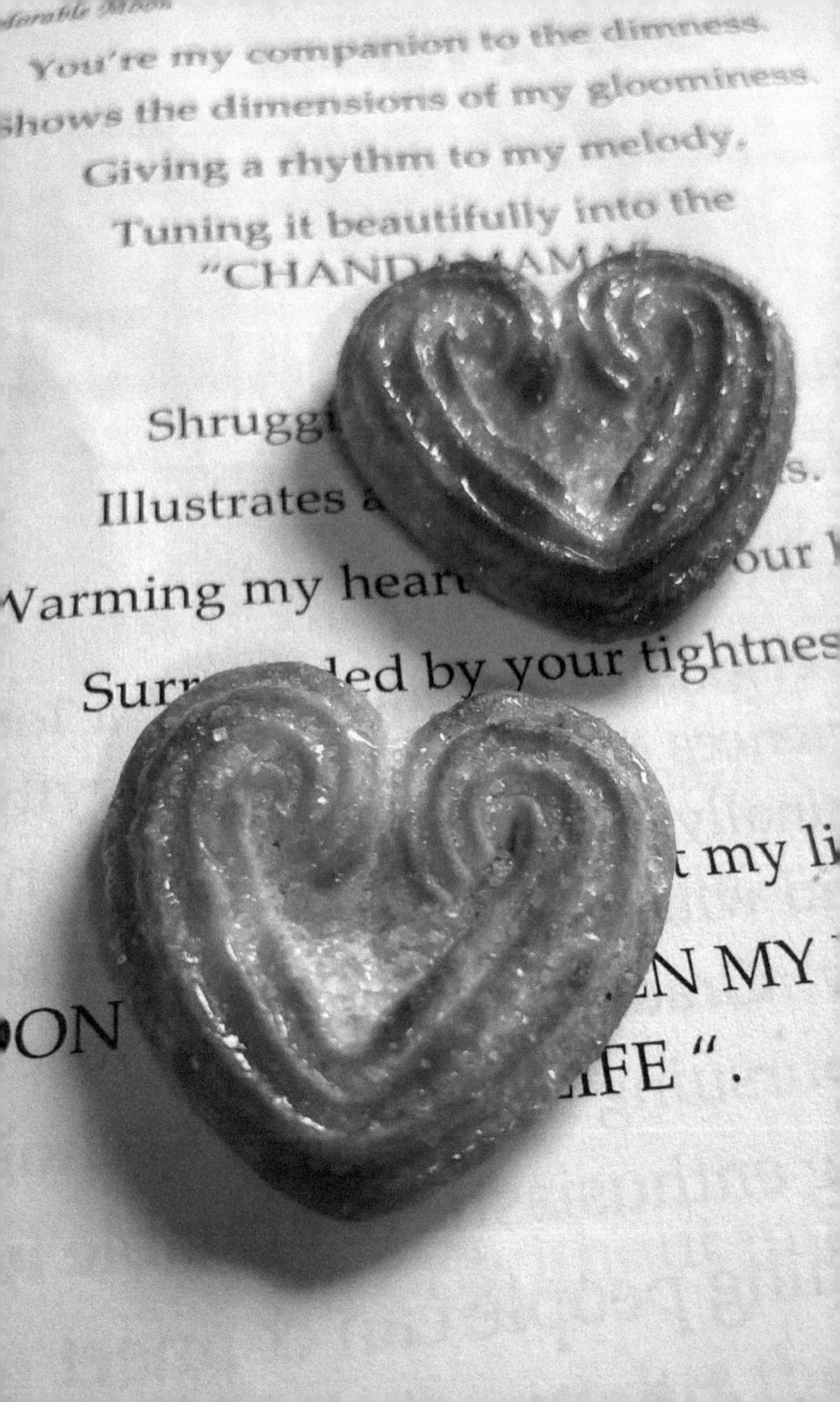

You're my companion to the dimness,
Shows the dimensions of my gloominess.
Giving a rhythm to my melody,
Tuning it beautifully into the
"CHAND

Shrugg
Illustrates a
Warming my hear
Surr

ded by your tightnes

ON

my li

N MY

FE ".

# I Heal a

With the rhymes
*i heal a*
*million heart,*
Penning down the
beauty through art .
Filling  myself with a
part of light ,
Being celestial in the
pot of life .


All i find is white ,
*so as my slight.*
Twilight's bright ,
*arousing my nights.*
enjoying the ignite ,
Despite being quite .


*Drowning in ink ,*
Pouring out what i think .
With the rhymes,
i heal a million heart.

# Driving amongst

Driving amongst
*the starry nights*
Along the brightening
lights ,
Travelling through
the gloomy moon & stars .

Clearing the pathways ,
Radiant beams of the highways ,
Dawning the bliss of the roads
Breezing the fog & snow.

Lowering the
*glasses,*
Rising up the
*music ,*
to enjoy ,
The mesmerising feels
of a midnight ride.

# Standing

Standing
*in front of water*
Seeing the shattered pieces
of my soul .
Drenching in the
rain ,
To hide the tears of
pain .
The fate of luck played
well ,
to be a fool to fell .


Burying the expectations of
*desire*
Being remained as a useless
*tire.*
Unsatisfied life covered like a
*shell,*
Waiting for the charm of success
*to ring a bell .*

# You're the

You're the symbolism of
*eternity* .
The bliss you add
to the
aroma of blue ,
decors the
reincarnation.

You're made
of hard core
*Gentle & Calm*
you wore .
Bringing
Postivity like the
deep oceans ,
Washing up the
negativity of desires.

# An Overwhelming emotion

The Overwhelming emotion
*that doesn't find words*,
appropriately
miraculous.
Setting the sky
Ablaze ,
Transforming the landscape
into a wonderland .
The bliss of the Autumn colour ,
Enchant the gloom of vision.

# I Stand

I Stand
*towering & prominent,*
Scrutinizing the welkin ,
with the tinge of elation.
*Spreading my wings*
*like a glad bird on*
*its flight,*
away from the glimpse
where ,
the light of nature
illumines the world within.
Playing their minstrel to assure ,
from the perils of uncertainity.

# Cumulus clouds

Cumulus clouds
*essentialising*
*across the welkin*
in fictional incarnation,
of varying shapes & sizes.
*Like a foam ocean*
me dance to the admisting,
*Like a candy floss,*
filled with the infinty of enticing .

# You're the

You're the

*fluffiest peace for this day*

winding like a

cumulus clouds for me .

Playing the

melodic symphony

by viewing the insights .

Blazing the

blissful of beauty of the soul ,

made me fall for you.

The drills drew nearer to you

every second ,

Bursting like the flicking

royal blue of spirit.

# As I Woke

As I Woke Up
*to be*
*beautiful*
*like a*
*blossom flower,*
looking up with passion.
My Heart smile
with love,
Which is a  perfect
insane .
Glazing the mushy
corolla
which  truly  made me
wonder ,
how the pretty
it  proved touched me .

# Running out

Running out

*of words*
*where everything seems*
*to be scary* .

The world

The people ,

Groaning deep within

Holding the breathe in a tin .

Life seems to be Terrific

Soaking in Horrific ,

& me becoming unspecific .

# Me

Is it me ?
The Questions of me
Rundown from the parallel  world .
When did i grow ?
When did i change ?
Water hides in the heart ,
Shattering the dreams apart.
My Mind Clogged ,
My Thoughts Bogged.
When did i develop  fears ?
When will  I be Okay ?
My Breath shallowed
My Present Followed
Is it me
or
The 20s soul
Who is Trying to  figure out
WHO SHE IS !

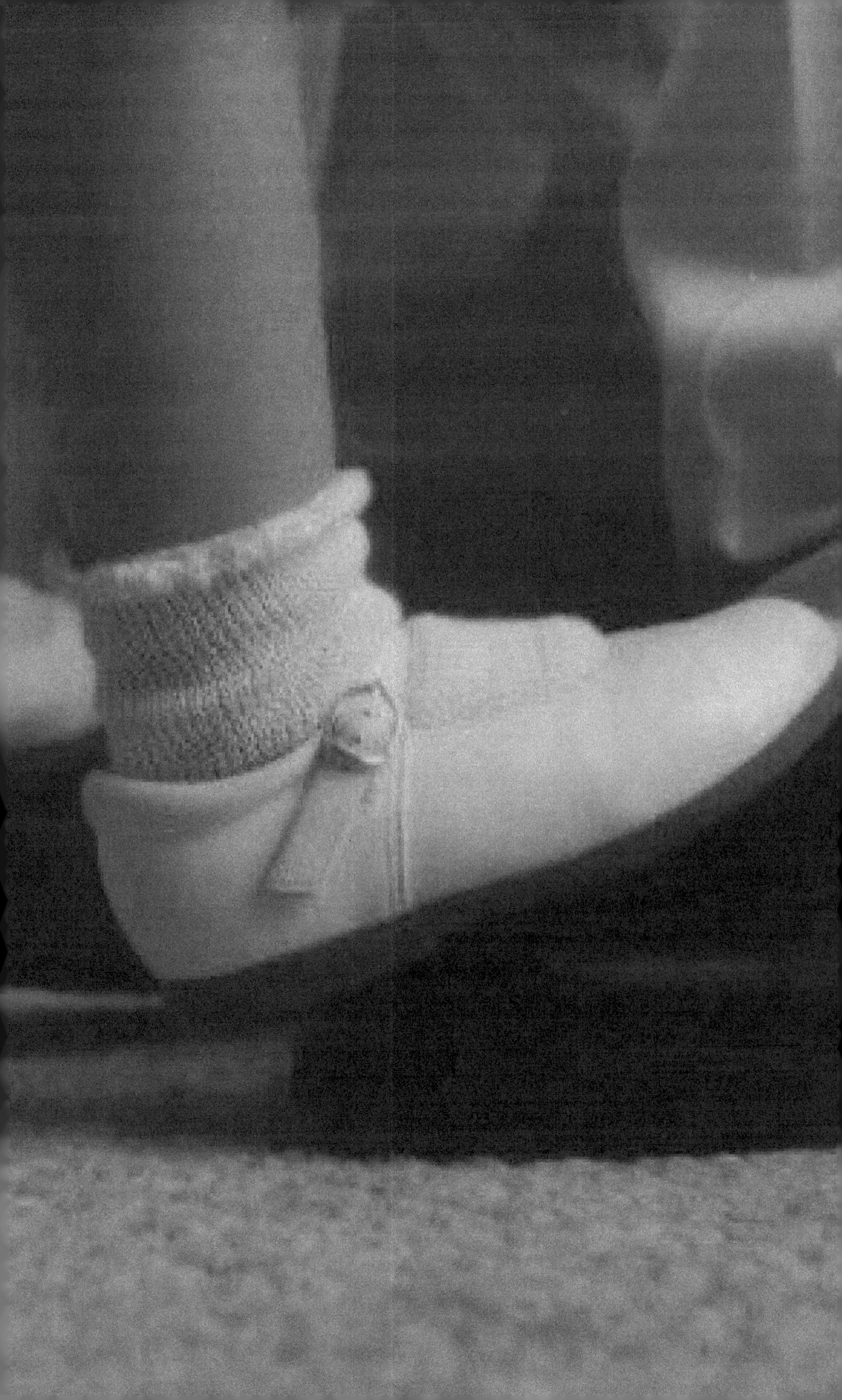

# I'm Stuck

I'm stuck
I'm stuck in
*between the Memories,*
I'm stuck
*between the Emotions.*
I'm stuck in this world ,
Where everything seems to be compact .
I'm stuck in managing the things,
That tilt  my head .
I'm stuck with packed thoughts ,
I'm stuck with compression .
I feel tired ,
I feel suffocated ,
I feel shattered
I feel I'm done with this feeling of Stucking life !

# I LOOK UP
# TO YOU

I Look up to you
with a tender heart,
&
blush on my face,
I Look up to you
with the eyes that sparkle
like a 1000 watt bulb,
I Look up to you
with a new hope of
finding myself.
I Look up to you
to heal my inner child
I Look , I Only look upon you
As your my blue to my Crew .

# Currently
# What could it be

What could it be the
*Name*,
What could it be the
*Same*,
What could it be the
*Game*,
Who can Remain ,
With
Unknown Future
Untold Frequencies
Unbundled Feelings
Unfolded emotions
By the sense of
Endearment .

# STUCK

Stuck in between the red light,
Warning the life to take a halt to make it right .
From the **Heart** ,
To the **Mind**
Filled with the
thoughts of confined.

Stuck in the middle to find,
To grind the Feelings of Combined,
From the body ,
To the soul ,
Filled with the spirit to **Bind**!

# BARE FEET

Bare feet
Baring the tilt .
Touching the Ground,
Bouncing the Wound.
Healing the Soul,
Peeling the Drool .
Wheeling the life ,
Adjusting the Drive .
Bare Feet
With the Hope of Being Straight !

# DESTINY & FATE

IS Writing the destiny is in our own hands
**- she asked**

I Had the Right to Write the destiny
**- Said Fate**

# OUT OF LOVE

Out of Love ,
*I take tricks & schemes ,*
in between the lines,
in between the gaps ,
Tender hide ,
with a Joyful ride .
Dancing in air ,
showering the flare.
Finding life in the
simpliest things
with a companion bliss .

KENNY HILLS
COFFEE

# IN A BOX


Can Tenderness &Tolerance be in a box
**~ He asked** ?
Can we prove ~ **She questioned** ?
What shall i write
**~ asked the poet** ?

# TO MANY THINGS

To many Things
to **HOLD**,
To many Things
to be **TOLD**.
To much
to **HANDLE** ,
To much
to be **RANDLED** .
What on
to **DANDLE** ,
What could it be
to be **TANGLED** .
After all Life is **A SCANDAL** !

# AN IMMOVABLE STATUE

I'm like an
immovable statue,
*Slowly melting away from
my dreams.*
As Hope makes her prisoner
Fate plays a Tale .
The chaos fills the mind ,
The broken wing inks the world .
I'm a story that never ends  ,
Just like the sun rises
EVERY NEW DAY !

# AS I RETURN

As i return

*to my Home,*

I see some

Personified beauty ,

Mesmerised beyond words ,

Enchanted by surplus .

# SHABBY ROADS

The shabby roads ,

The cool breeze,

Wrapped up in peace ,

Melted to be Pleased,

To witness the Rainy day's

Masterpiece.

# WE HOLD

We Hold

We Hold a lot of things that

are buried beyond.

To Hold & Behold the cold

To be Told To Sold ,

The unfolding folds of life.

# A WILD FLOWER

A Wild flower among the

*Blues*,

As I walk Around the

*Views*,

Moving The way by the

*Cues*

In a loop Full of

*Booms!*

# A COMPANION TO TREAT

As I walk Down the

*Street*

I found a Companion to

*Treat.*

with the light ,

along the narrow road straight .

going deep within  the spright

clearing the vision bright .

Beauty along with the upright ,

leaping around the Twlight .

Enhanced that

I found My Companion for tonight !

# A TWLIGHT

Twlight

*Light,*

Arousing the spirit

*Bright.*

The Warmth ,

The ease of

*Comfort,*

That i found myself

*Tight.*

Holding Around the arms ,

Igniting the blown charms .

Delighted by the calm ,

*This is what the beauty of your*

*Soul Right !*

# TOO MANY

To Many

Prayers

To Many

Sorrows,

To Many

Broken Hearts,

To Many

Screams,

To Many

Tears.

Too Many Things to say,

Too Many Things to Hear.

Too Many To Be Healed,

Too Many To Be Solved.

There Are too Many !